The KidHaven Science Library

The Sun

by Peggy J. Parks

KIDHAVEN PRESS

An imprint of Thomson Gale, a part of The Thomson Corporation

THOMSON

GALE

Detroit • New York • San Francisco • New Haven, Conn. • Waterville, Maine • London

© 2008 Thomson Gale, a part of The Thomson Corporation.

Thomson and Star Logo are trademarks and Gale and KidHaven Press are registered trademarks used herein under license.

For more information, contact
KidHaven Press
27500 Drake Rd.
Farmington Hills, MI 48331-3535
Or you can visit our Internet site at http://www.gale.com

LIBRARY OF CONGRESS CATALOGING-IN-PUBLICATION DATA

Parks, Peggy J., 1951–
   The sun / by Peggy J. Parks.
      p. cm. — (KidHaven science library)
   Includes bibliographical references and index.
   ISBN-13: 978-0-7377-3778-3 (hardcover)
   1. Sun—Juvenile literature. I. Title.
   QB521.5.P376 2008
   523.7—dc22

                                                                2007022034

ISBN-10: 0-7377-3778-6

Printed in the United States of America

Contents

Chapter 1
Earth's Star 4

Chapter 2
The Sun and Living Things 12

Chapter 3
Marvels in the Sky 20

Chapter 4
Solar Exploration 30

Notes. 40

Glossary 42

For Further Exploration 43

Index. 45

Picture Credits 47

About the Author 48

Earth's Star

Although the Sun may not twinkle in the night-time sky, it is a star. It is actually a rather ordinary star—bigger and hotter than some, smaller and cooler than others. What makes the Sun unique is that it is Earth's star. Even at 93 million miles (150 million km) away, it is thousands of times closer to our planet than any other star.

The Birth of the Sun

In many ways the Sun is a mystery to scientists. But after studying it for years, they have learned a great deal about it. They believe it started to form about 5 billion years ago. Like all stars, the Sun began as a giant whirling cloud of gas and dust called a **nebula**.

As more space debris collected in the nebula, it became heavier. It began spinning faster and faster. Finally its own gravity pulled most of the gas and dust particles into a tight cluster in the center. The gases in the center became very hot, and pressure began to build up. Then there was a massive, blinding explosion. A brilliant new star known as the Sun had come to life.

Layers of Gas

When the Sun appears in the daytime sky, it is difficult to imagine how enormous it is. Its diameter is about 865,000 miles (1.4 million km). If the Sun were hollow, more than a million Earths could fit inside it! The Sun has separate layers, which scientists sometimes refer to as shells. Because it is made entirely of gas, the Sun has no solid surface.

The two main regions of the Sun are the interior and the solar atmosphere. At the very center of the interior is the **core**. Scientists believe that it is more than 100,000 miles (161,000km) thick. The core is extremely dense, or tightly packed. Above the core is the radiative zone, and outside that is the convective zone. Gigantic columns of gas in the convective zone carry solar energy outward toward the

The Sun was a nebula before it became a star.

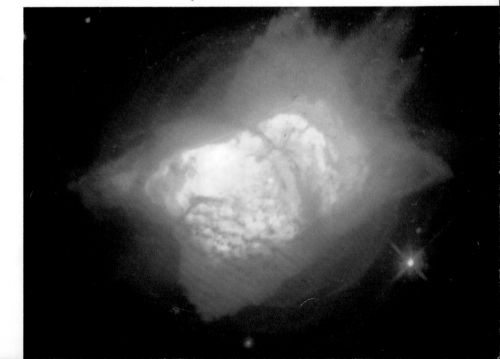

surface. Scientist and author Jack Zirker explains: "Bubbles of hot gas, the size of Alaska, rise to the surface, radiate their heat, and sink back to the depths."[1]

Surrounding the Sun's interior is its atmosphere, which has three layers. The innermost layer is the **photosphere**, meaning "sphere of light." The photosphere is often referred to as the surface of the Sun. It is about 400 miles (600km) thick—about as thick as the state of California is long. It is also the part of the Sun that scientists are most able to observe and study. Within the photosphere, solar gases furiously bubble and churn. This causes the

The other planets in the solar system seem tiny compared to the enormous size of the Sun (lower right).

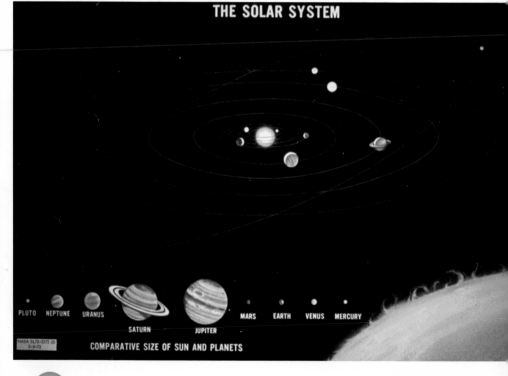

THE SOLAR SYSTEM

PLUTO   NEPTUNE   URANUS   MARS   EARTH   VENUS   MERCURY

SATURN   JUPITER

NASA SL72-2272 (3)
2-9-72   COMPARATIVE SIZE OF SUN AND PLANETS

The dark, patchy areas on the surface of the Sun are called sunspots.

Sun to wobble, as the Stanford Solar Center Web site explains: "The Sun vibrates up and down, in and out, much like a pot of fudge boiling on the stove. When you make fudge, you can see large bubbles of chocolate covering the pan. And in each of those big bubbles you can also see a set of tiny bubbles growing and popping with gusto. The Sun is the same."[2] Another quality of the photosphere is its **sunspots**. These areas can grow to be 60,000 miles (97,000km) in diameter. Scientists believe they are caused by disturbances in the Sun's magnetic field.

The layer surrounding the photosphere is the **chromosphere**. It is about 1,550 miles (2,500km) thick, but it cannot be seen because of the blinding light of the photosphere beneath it. The chromosphere merges into the **corona**, which is the outermost region of the Sun's atmosphere. The corona extends millions of miles into outer space.

Nuclear Space Furnace

The Sun is unbelievably hot, but it does not burn like wood burns. Its heat comes from **nuclear fusion** in the core. This is created when the core's immense heat and pressure cause changes in the Sun's gases. The atoms that make up hydrogen gas constantly bump into each other. Their centers, or **nuclei**, fuse (join) together. This fusion creates a massive amount of energy—as much as the explosions of 100 billion hydrogen bombs per second!

Temperatures in the Sun vary in the different layers. The core is by far the hottest part. It can soar to 27 million °F (15 million °C). In comparison, a roaring fire on Earth burns at only about 2,000°F (1,093°C). Science journalist April Holladay describes the core's immense heat: "A grain of sand this hot would cook a person 90 miles (145km) away."[3]

The Sun's atmosphere is also extremely hot, but it has a peculiar quality. Even though the core is the hottest zone, the layers closest to it are cooler than the outer layers. For example, the photosphere averages almost 11,000°F (6,100°C). In the chromosphere, which extends for several thousand miles (kilometers) above the photosphere, temperatures are about 54,000°F (30,000°C). Still farther out in the corona, temperatures are more than a million degrees F (560,000°C). Scientists have studied this in depth, and they still do not understand it. Zirker explains: "Why the atmosphere's temperature rises in this way is one of the most challenging questions astronomers are trying to answer."[4]

Equally puzzling to astronomers, or scientists who study the sky, is why the corona grows hotter

The corona, shown in an X-ray photo, is the outermost region of the Sun's atmosphere.

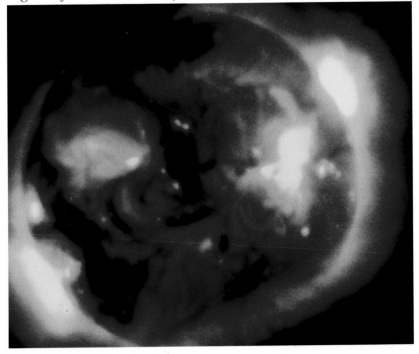

the farther it stretches out in space. Temperatures at the layer's outer edges have reached as high as 3.6 million °F (2 million °C).

A Spinning Star

Another unusual solar quality is known as **differential rotation**. Like planets, the Sun rotates around an imaginary line known as an axis. But because it is made of gas, it rotates at different rates of speed. Harvard scientists Leon Golub and Jay M. Pasachoff explain: "An ordinary globe rotates as a solid body: when you spin the globe, all of its parts take the same amount of time to complete a rotation. This is not the case for the Sun."[5] The point near the Sun's equator takes about 27 days to make a complete rotation. The Sun's north and south poles rotate more slowly. It takes these areas about 32 days to make a complete rotation.

At the same time that the Sun is rotating on its axis, Earth and other planets are constantly circling it in their orbits. This happens because of gravity. The Sun's massive size creates an extremely strong gravitational pull. The National Aeronautics and Space Administration (NASA) explains: "The sun . . . plays the role of a big anchor, which creates gravity that keeps our planet and the other planets of the solar system in a small space. If it weren't for the sun, our planet would simply fly off loose into the universe."[6]

The Sun (center) rotates at different rates of speed.

Earth's star is as fascinating as it is mysterious. For 5 billion years, it has been bathing the planet with light and warmth. Although the Sun is still puzzling to scientists, they have learned a great deal about it. In the future, they will continue to study the skies in an effort to learn more.

Chapter 2

The Sun and Living Things

For thousands of years, humans have known that the Sun makes life possible on Earth. In many ancient cultures, people worshipped the Sun. The Egyptians believed that their sun god, Ra, was the creator of all things. The ancient Greeks worshipped a sun god named Helios. They believed that he drove a golden chariot and moved the Sun across the sky every day. In ancient China, people respected the Sun's power so much, they believed there were ten suns.

Food from the Sun

Although beliefs about the Sun have changed since ancient times, most people know that it is essential for life. The Sun provides Earth with an enormous amount of energy, as Zirker explains: "In one second the sun emits enough energy to supply the United States for *four million years*!"[7]

Living things depend on the Sun's energy for many reasons. One of the most important is that it helps plants grow. All plants take up energy from the Sun. They combine it with carbon dioxide in the air and water from the soil to make sugars for their food. This is a process known as **photosynthesis**.

Because plants are at the bottom of the **food chain**, they are the basis for all the food in the world. The food chain is the relationship between living organisms that depend on each other for survival. It starts with grass, roots, and other plant materials that are food for small animals that do not eat meat, such as rabbits and mice. Larger meat-eating predators eat the smaller animals. The food chain continues as those creatures are eaten by even bigger animals.

Experiments show that the amount of sunlight plants are exposed to determines how fast they will grow.

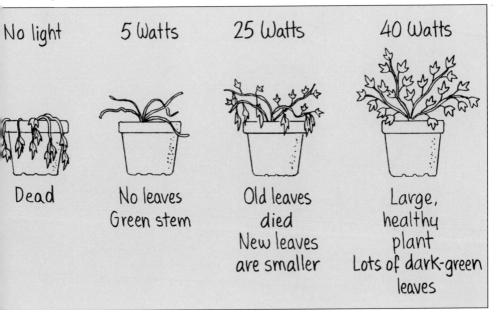

No light — Dead

5 Watts — No leaves Green stem

25 Watts — Old leaves died New leaves are smaller

40 Watts — Large, healthy plant Lots of dark-green leaves

In oceans, lakes, and streams, the food chain begins with algae and microscopic plants that grow in water. The plants are eaten by small fish, which are eaten by larger, predator fish. At the very top of the food chain are humans. Whether they eat plants, animals, or fish, all of their food is made possible by the Sun.

The Sun and Its Partners

In addition to making plants grow, the Sun also keeps Earth warm. Without it, the planet would be nothing more than a dark, frozen wasteland where

The food chain is the relationship between living organisms that depend on each other for survival.

no life could exist. The atmosphere works with the Sun to control the climate. It is a blanket of mixed gases that wraps around Earth. It keeps the planet from becoming too hot by letting in only a certain amount of sunlight. It also protects Earth from becoming too cold. When the Sun shines on Earth, part of its heat is absorbed by land and water. The rest is reflected away from the surface. But all of the heat does not escape into space. Some of it is captured and held by the atmosphere. This is similar to the way a greenhouse works, so it is known as the **greenhouse effect**.

Golub and Pasachoff explain the importance of the Sun and atmosphere working together in this way:

> From the point of view of climate, Earth is basically a large rock floating in cold, empty space with an enormously bright searchlight shining on one side of it. If Earth did not rotate and did not have an atmosphere, then the side being illuminated would be hotter than boiling water and the dark side would be solidly frozen. A rotating Earth would be more evenly heated, like a rotisserie chicken being cooked, but without an atmosphere the *average* temperature around the globe would still be below the freezing point of water. The warming . . . known as the greenhouse effect, is necessary to keep the Earth [livable].[8]

Like a greenhouse, Earth's atmosphere helps keep the Sun's heat from escaping into space.

The Sun has another partner in controlling climate: the oceans. Nearly three-fourths of Earth's surface is covered in seawater. Because the oceans are so enormous, their deep, dark waters absorb far more of the Sun's energy than land does. Also, oceans help control the climate through evaporation. When water evaporates, it becomes a gas known as water vapor. It rises into the atmosphere and cools. It then falls to the Earth as rain or snow. Water vapor also joins other gases in the atmosphere. Of all these gases, water vapor is the most powerful at trapping and storing the Sun's heat.

The World's Extremes

Although the Sun warms the entire planet, some areas of the world get much less sunlight than others. For example, the North Pole, also called the Arctic, is covered in darkness during the winter. The sun sets in the autumn and does not rise again until spring. This is caused by the way the planet is tilted. In the winter, the North Pole is tilted farther away from the Sun than any other area of the world. As a result, sunlight strikes the land at a less direct angle. Months of complete darkness drag on and on. When spring finally arrives, the North Pole has tilted back toward the Sun. The Sun rises and does not set again until autumn. There are weeks and weeks of constant daylight. That is why the Arctic is often called the Land of the Midnight Sun.

The South Pole, or Antarctica, experiences the same thing—only in reverse. When it is summer at the North Pole, it is winter at the South Pole. Antarctic winters are even harsher than those at the Arctic. The coldest temperature ever recorded on Earth was in Antarctica. In July 1983, a Russian weather station in East Antarctica recorded temperatures of -129°F (-89.4°C).

Hostile Planets

Winters at the poles are cold, dark, and harsh. But even the worst climate on Earth is far better than that on planets farther away from the Sun.

Neptune, for example, is 2.8 billion miles (4.5 billion km) from the Sun. From the planet's surface, the Sun appears as just another star in the sky. Because the Sun is so far away, Neptune is extremely cold. Temperatures can fall to -400°F (-240°C). No life could ever survive in such a hostile climate.

There are also hostile conditions on planets that are closer to the Sun. At 36 million miles (58 mil-

Neptune (pictured) can reach temperatures as low as -400°F.

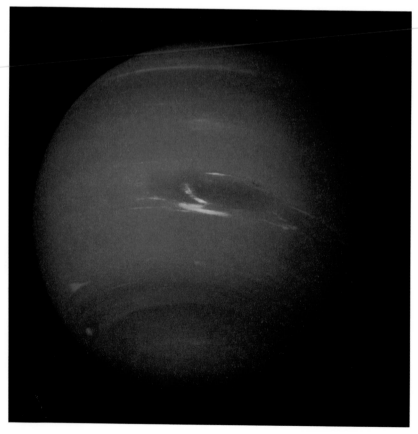

lion km) away, Mercury is the Sun's closest neighbor. NASA explains how this looks in the sky: "Imagine looking up at a Sun that is three times larger than what you see on Earth. That is how our Sun would look on Mercury."[9] During the day, the temperature on Mercury can reach as high as 800 °F (427°C). But there are extreme swings in temperature, because the planet has almost no atmosphere and thus no way to hold the Sun's heat. Mercury's temperature can vary by more than 1,000 °F (530°C) between day and night.

Unlike Mercury, Venus does have an atmosphere. It is poisonous and extremely thick. It is also heavy—so heavy that it would immediately crush anything on the surface, even a tough metal spacecraft. Venus is farther away from the Sun than Mercury is. Because of its atmosphere, however, it is a hotter planet. Its atmosphere traps and holds the Sun's great heat. As a result, temperatures there can soar to more than 900°F (482°C).

The Sun makes life on Earth possible. It provides heat, light, and food. It heats the land, oceans, and air. It works with the atmosphere to keep the climate pleasant, rather than scorching hot or freezing cold. Because of the Sun, Earth is a place where living things can thrive.

Chapter 3

Marvels in the Sky

In addition to giving life to Earth, the Sun also makes the sky dance with light and color. From brilliantly colored rainbows to crimson and gold sunsets, people marvel at the beauty that sunlight creates.

Painted Skies

Earth's atmosphere works with the Sun to create stunning creations. The Stanford Solar Center explains: "The Sun and our atmosphere are a magical and mischievous team, often trying to trick us with unlikely appearances."[10]

One of those tricks is the blue color of the sky, which is actually a product of scattered light. When the Sun shines down, it appears to be colorless. But it is actually a mixture of a whole range of colors known as the spectrum. As colorful as the spectrum is, when all the colors are combined they look white—which creates sunlight's colorless look. The colors become separated when the Sun shines through the atmosphere. Its light bumps into dust, ice crystals, pollen, and other tiny particles of matter. This causes the light to scatter all over the sky, which means the colors scatter too. Blue light spreads out more than red and other colors. So during the daytime, the skies appear to be blue.

This same scattering of light creates an illusion that the Sun is red in the early morning and at dusk. These are called "sunrise" and "sunset," even though it is

At dusk, a sunset occurs as the Sun appears to drop below the horizon.

Earth that moves, rather than the Sun. At daybreak, the planet is rotating toward the Sun. At dusk, it is rotating away. During both of these times, the Sun appears close to the horizon. That means its light must travel at an angle. It must also cover a longer distance than it does during the day. Again, the sunlight shines through debris in the atmosphere. The blue light is bent away from the horizon. It must scatter over a greater distance, so it can no longer be seen. Red, yellow, and orange scatter more slowly. They are left behind to paint the horizon with color.

Arches of Color

Sometimes the sky is painted with many colors, such as when a rainbow appears. Author Donald Ahrens describes a rainbow as "one of the most spectacular light shows observed on earth."[11] For a rainbow to form, both rain and sunlight are needed. During a rainstorm, the sky is thick with clouds. When the Sun finally shines through, its bright light passes through millions of raindrops. They act like tiny pieces of glass known as prisms, which split light into its various colors. These millions of rain prisms reflect a brilliant fan of colors against the sky.

Sometimes mini-rainbows appear. On a bright, sunny day, sunlight shines through the mist of a fountain or a garden sprinkler. These droplets of water also act like prisms, creating a tiny rainbow in the air.

A rainbow emerges from both rain and sunlight.

Halos and Sun Dogs

Another of the Sun's colorful creations usually forms before a storm. It is called a sun halo, which is a ring of light that encircles the Sun. When a storm is approaching, wispy clouds known as cirrus clouds begin moving in. The ice crystals that make up the clouds bend sunlight. This causes the Sun to look as though it is surrounded by a glowing halo. Sun halos are often red on the inside of the circle and blue on the outside.

A similar phenomenon of sunlight is known as a sun dog. These bright patches of light also form when cirrus clouds are present. But unlike halos, sun dogs are only a small part of a circle. They may form as part of a halo, or on their own. Sometimes sun dogs are on just one side of the Sun. Or, they may appear on both sides. They are usually most visible just before the Sun sets in the western sky.

Shimmering Sky Lights

Of all the beauty that is created by sunlight, **auroras** are some of the most stunning. These bright, colorful bands of light are named after Aurora, the Roman goddess of dawn. They are best seen during the winter months in areas above the Arctic Circle, such as northern Alaska and Canada. There they are often called the Northern Lights. Auroras also appear in Antarctica during the winter and are often referred to as the Southern Lights. Wherever

Sundogs can be seen over a snow-covered field in Minnesota.

they appear, auroras shimmer, sparkle, and glow like jewels. They light up the sky with wispy flowing curtains of red, green, and blue light.

Auroras begin with powerful explosions on the Sun. These explosions usually occur in giant sunspots, which have strong magnetic fields. After such a blast, a massive cloud of super-heated gas

Aurora borealis, also known as the Northern Lights, is one of nature's most spectacular displays of light.

billows out from the Sun. This is known as a **solar wind** or solar flare. The cloud zooms through space up to 2 million miles per hour (3.2 million kph). It carries magnetic fields and charged particles along with it. When the cloud reaches Earth's atmosphere, most of the particles inside it are screened out by Earth's own protective magnetic field. The particles that make it through the atmosphere slam into gases. These collisions cause the gases to release light, and a glistening aurora appears in the sky.

"An Awesome Experience"

Another amazing view in the sky occurs when the Sun disappears. This is known as a total solar eclipse. It happens when the Moon, which is orbiting Earth, passes directly in front of the Sun. Of course, the Sun is millions of times larger than the Moon. But because the Sun is so much farther away in space, it looks no larger when viewed from Earth.

A solar flare erupts on the surface of the Sun after a powerful explosion.

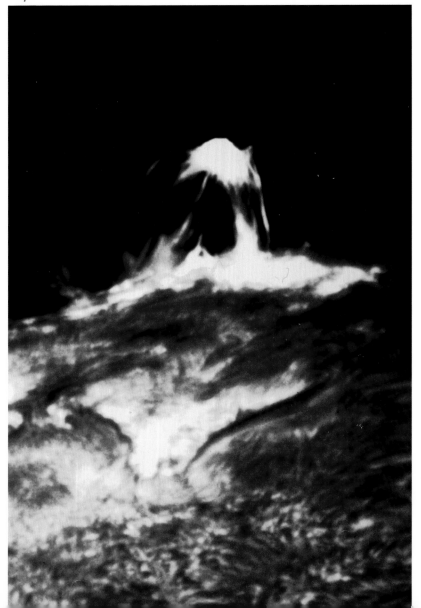

During a total eclipse, the dark disk of the Moon blocks out all sunlight. This can look eerie, because a bright, sunny day suddenly becomes very dark. But it is also a beautiful thing to see. A total solar eclipse provides a rare opportunity to view the Sun's corona shining against the dark sky. Because of the beauty of eclipses, people often travel thousands of miles to see them. Science writer Bill Arnett explains: "To stand in the shadow of the Moon is an awesome experience. For a few precious minutes it gets dark in the middle of the day. The stars come out. The animals and birds think it's time to go to sleep. And you can see the solar corona. It is well worth a major journey."[12]

Not all solar eclipses block out the sun completely. During some eclipses the Moon covers only part of the Sun. A partial eclipse occurs when the Moon passes in front of the Sun, but does not hide it completely. When that happens, the Sun looks like a giant cookie with a bite taken out of it.

The Sun completely disappears from view during a solar eclipse.

Another type is known as an annular eclipse, which happens when the Moon is farther out in its orbit around Earth. The distance makes the Moon appear to be slightly smaller than the Sun. As with a total eclipse, when an annular eclipse occurs, the Moon is directly in front of the Sun. But because it looks smaller, a ring of sunlight appears around it like a halo.

Blue skies, brilliant rainbows, shimmering auroras, and eclipses are just a few of the wonders created by the Sun. When people gaze at the sky, they are in awe of the majestic beauty before their eyes.

Chapter 4

Solar Exploration

Astronomers have been studying the Sun throughout the centuries. In the early 1600s, an Italian scientist named Galileo Galilei built an instrument that became known as the telescope. Galileo's telescope was a primitive device, and the images he saw through it were fuzzy. But he was able to observe sunspots on the Sun's surface. He also confirmed what a few astronomers before him had suspected—that the Sun was still while Earth and other planets orbited it. This was known as a **heliocentric** theory, and it challenged established beliefs.

Galileo was severely punished for making his ideas public. But in the following years, he was proven correct. His telescope—and his findings about the Sun's relationship to the planets—brought about a new era of solar exploration. NASA astronomer Madhulika Guhathakurta explains why solar exploration is so important: "Of the bazillion stars that we have in our night sky, the sun is the only one that counts. Any understanding or breakthrough we can make in understanding the sun and the sun's environment is of direct relevance to every human being on this planet."[13]

Observing the Sun from Earth

Astronomers such as Guhathakurta have an amazing variety of complex instruments to study the Sun and other stars. The telescopes they use are enormous and powerful. But because the Sun's light is both blinding and dangerous, they must use special filters to protect their eyes.

Some of the largest and most powerful telescopes in the world are at the National Solar Observatory

Galileo's observations helped to prove the Sun-centered model of the solar system.

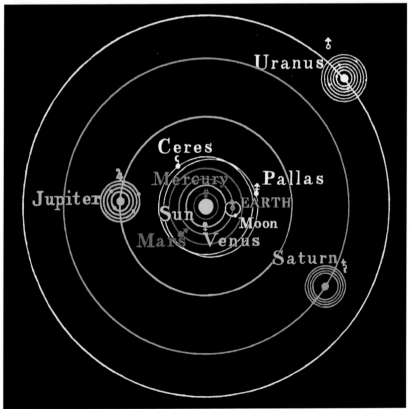

in Sunspot, New Mexico. On December 11, 2006, astronomers at the observatory saw an unusual phenomenon. There was a gigantic explosion on the Sun, which was triggered by a powerful shock wave. Astronomers said the blast occurred in a sunspot that was as big as the entire Earth. They

In 2006 scientists witnessed a solar tsunami, a giant explosion on the surface of the Sun.

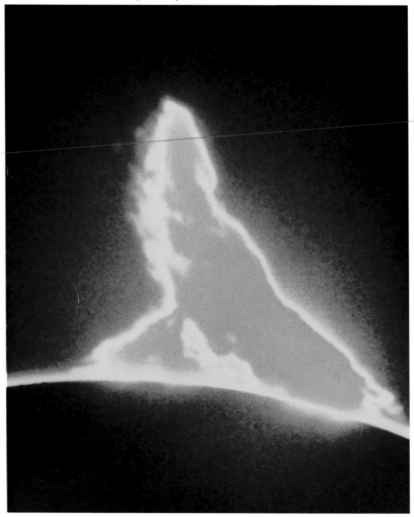

watched the fiery blast flare up and then roll across the Sun's surface. They compared the disturbance to a tsunami on Earth. Tsunamis are giant sea waves that usually occur after underwater earthquakes. Just as tsunamis race through the ocean, the solar tsunami roared across the Sun's surface—traveling at about 700,000 miles per hour (1.1 million kph)! Astronomers said they had never seen anything like it before.

Solar Studies from Space

After observing the solar tsunami, astronomers said it was unusual to see such an event from telescopes on the ground. That is because the instruments encounter obstacles from Earth's atmosphere. The atmosphere is so thick that it distorts, or bends, the light from the Sun and other stars. As their light beams toward Earth, the atmosphere distorts how it looks. NASA explains: "The visual effect of this distortion is like looking at an object through a glass of water. Telescopes here on the ground—which also must peer through Earth's atmosphere—are equally vulnerable to our atmosphere's visual tricks."[14]

To address this challenge, astronomers often study the Sun from space. Spacecraft such as the Solar and Heliospheric Observatory (SOHO) orbit the Sun and record information about it. SOHO orbits the Sun as though it were a planet. It keeps a close watch so astronomers have an uninterrupted view. The spacecraft is equipped with more than a dozen solar observation instruments. Each of the instruments is designed to study a different aspect of the Sun.

Since SOHO was first launched in December 1995, it has provided a wealth of new information. The spacecraft has captured images of sunspots, which has helped scientists gain a better understanding of their structure. It has measured solar winds and calculated how fast they travel. It has seen currents of gas flowing beneath the layers of the photosphere. It has discovered that the Sun's magnetic fields often change rapidly. It has also recorded detailed information about the Sun's corona, which astronomers now know has its own weather. NASA explains: "SOHO has observed explosions, remarkable shock waves, and tornado-like storms there."[15]

"A New Era of Study"

A spacecraft launched by Japan in September 2006 is also helping astronomers gain new knowledge about the Sun. The craft is called *Hinode*, which is the Japanese word for "sunrise." *Hinode*'s main mission is to observe explosive activity on the Sun. It will study the solar magnetic field and record information about how energy moves from the core outward to the corona. Its three high-powered telescopes will study the Sun's various layers. Cameras

This image of the Sun was
taken by the Solar and
Heliospheric Observatory.

on the instruments provide crystal-clear images for astronomers to analyze.

Within a few months of its launch, *Hinode* began to send valuable information to scientists back on Earth. It captured greatly magnified views of the Sun's surface. This allowed scientists to observe hot solar gases constantly rising and falling through the atmosphere. They received data that would help

This image of the Sun and its corona was taken by the Japanese spacecraft, Hinode.

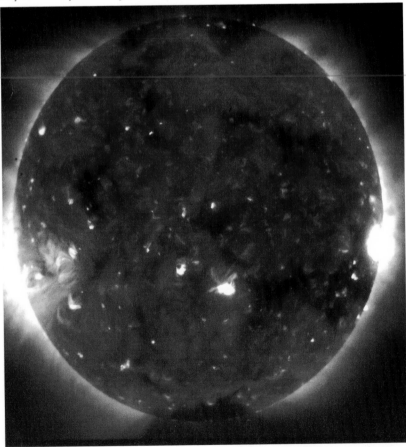

them more accurately determine the temperature of the Sun's layers, including its atmosphere. Of particular interest was the information *Hinode* provided about the Sun's magnetic fields. Images showed a "boiling cauldron of swaying spikes."[16] Some of these towering spikes of magnetism were 5,000 miles (8,000km) long. *Hinode* also produced some surprising discoveries. Scientists had long suspected that there were twisted, tangled magnetic fields on the Sun, but they thought the fields traveled outward. *Hinode* showed gigantic magnetic loops crashing in the other direction—onto the Sun's surface.

According to NASA scientist Dick Fisher, *Hinode* will provide information about the Sun that has never been known before. He explains: "These images will open a new era of study on some of the sun's processes that [affect] Earth, astronauts, orbiting satellites and the solar system."[17]

The Sun's Fate

One of the things that scientists have determined from studying the Sun is that it will not last forever. Its lifespan has been calculated to be about 10 billion years. Because it has been burning for half of that time, it has about 5 billion years left.

That is when the core will run out of fuel. The Sun's massive gravity will force all of its mass inward toward the core. As the core continues to

Eventually, the Sun will collapse and become a white dwarf star like the one pictured here.

shrink, it will become hotter and hotter. This will heat the outer layers, causing them to expand. The Sun will appear to be bigger and brighter in the sky than ever before. Eventually, it will become a dying star known as a **red giant**.

April Holladay describes the Sun's final phase: "The Sun will [still be] hot enough to burn planets to cinders as it engulfs Mercury and Venus and scorches Earth. Finally, a couple of billion years later, it will run out of all fuel and collapse into a tiny (Earth-size) hot **white dwarf** that will shine as a moon-bright diamond in our skies."[18]

Ever since Galileo studied the skies with his telescope, solar exploration has provided valuable information about the Sun. As even more sophisticated technology is developed, many of its remaining mysteries may be solved. But even though much has been learned about Earth's star, scientists say they still have a long way to go before they fully understand the Sun. NASA explains: "The sun is a fascinating star. Even though humans have been watching it for thousands of years, it still finds new ways to surprise us."[19]

Notes

Chapter 1: Earth's Star

1. Jack B. Zirker, *Journey from the Center of the Sun*. Princeton, NJ: Princeton University Press, 2002, p. 10.
2. Stanford Solar Center. http://solar-center.Stanford.edu/singing/singing.htm.
3. April Holladay, "Discovering the Sun's Center, How Big the Sun, Silver Among the Gold," *USA Today*, April 30, 2004. www.usatoday.com/tech/columnist/aprilholladay/2004-04-29-wonderquest_x.htm.
4. Zirker, *Journey from the Center of the Sun*, p.11.
5. Leon Golub and Jay M. Pasachoff, *Nearest Star*. Cambridge, MA: Harvard University Press, 2001, p. 113.
6. NASA, "Why Do We Study the Sun?" *Sun for Kids*. www.nasa.gov/vision/universe/solarsystem/sun_for_kids_main.html.

Chapter 2: The Sun and Living Things

7. Zirker, *Journey from the Center of the Sun*, p. 8.
8. Golub and Pasachoff, *Nearest Star*, p. 182.
9. NASA, "Mercury: The Swiftest Planet," NASA's *Solar System Exploration*. http://sse.jpl.nasa.gov/planets/profile.cfm?Display=Kids&Object=Mercury.

Chapter 3: Marvels in the Sky

10. Stanford Solar Center, "The Sun on Earth." http://solar-center.Stanford.edu/sun-on-earth.earth.html.
11. Quoted in Beverly Lynds, "About Rainbows," The National Center for Atmospheric Research & the UCAR Office of Programs. http://eo.ucar.edu/rainbows.

12. Bill Arnett, "The Sun," *Nine Planets,* August 25, 2006. www.nineplanets.org/sol.html.

Chapter 4: Solar Exploration

13. Quoted in Mike Schneider, "NASA Spacecraft to Study Solar Flares," *King County (WA) Journal,* October 26, 2006.
14. NASA HubbleSite Reference Desk. www.hubblesite.org/reference_desk.
15. NASA, "SOHO Image of the Sun," *NASAexplores,* February 3, 2005. www.nasaexplores/com/show2_article a.php?id=05-102.
16. Roger Highfield, "Images Show Sun in New Light," *Telegraph (London),* March 22, 2007. www. telegraph. co.uk/connected/main.jhtml?xml=/connected/2007/03/22/nsun122.xml.
17. Quoted in Highfield, "Images Show Sun in New Light."
18. Holladay, "Discovering the Sun's Center, How Big the Sun, Silver Among the Gold."
19. NASA, "SOHO Image of the Sun."

Glossary

auroras: Colorful displays of light in the sky.

chromosphere: The layer of solar atmosphere between the photosphere and the corona.

core: The innermost part of the Sun.

corona: The Sun's outer atmospheric layer.

differential rotation: The way the Sun rotates at different speeds.

food chain: The relationship between living organisms that depend on each other for survival.

greenhouse effect: The ability of Earth's atmosphere to hold and trap the Sun's heat.

heliocentric: Revolving around the Sun.

nebula: A massive whirling cloud of gas and dust.

nuclear fusion: The process that occurs when heat and pressure cause changes in gases.

nuclei: The central core of atoms.

photosphere: The lowest layer of the Sun's atmosphere (also called the surface of the Sun).

photosynthesis: The process by which plants combine the Sun's energy with carbon dioxide and water to make sugars for their food.

red giant: An old star whose size has massively expanded.

solar wind: A massive hot cloud of gas that results from a solar explosion.

sunspots: Dark patches on the Sun's surface.

white dwarf: The last remnant of a dying star.

For Further Exploration

Books

Ian Ridpath, *Stars and Planets Atlas*. New York: Facts On File, 2005. This atlas explains space-related phenomena, including the Sun and its relationship to planets.

Carole Stott, *Curious Kids Guides: Space*. New York: Kingfisher, 2002. This book includes many facts about the solar system, including how stars form and how long it takes planets to orbit the Sun.

Visual Encyclopedia of Space. New York: Dorling Kindersley Children, 2006. Using full-color photographs, illustrations, diagrams, and charts this book helps readers learn about space.

Periodicals

Francis Downey, "Sky Lights," *National Geographic Explorer*, April 2006, pp. 18–23.

Science Made Simple, "Learn More About: Planets & Their Orbits," October 2005, pp. 5–6.

Science Made Simple, "What Is a Star? Why Do Stars Shine?" February 2004, pp. 1–4.

Kathy Wollard, "Sun's Orbital Comfort Zone Is Limited," *Eye on Science*, December 26, 2002.

Internet Resources

E. Sohn, "A Dead Star's Dusty Ring," *Science News for Kids*, February 21, 2007. www.sciencenewsforkids.org/articles/20070221/Note2.asp.

E. Sohn, "Tracking Solar Storms," *Science News for Kids*, March 7, 2007. www.sciencenewsforkids.org/articles/20070307/Note3.asp.

Web Sites

Astronomy Magazine, Intro to the Sky (www.astronomy. com/asy/default.aspx?c=ss&id=157). This site is packed with information about the Sun and other stars, auroras, meteors, and sunspots. Also features a special section for young people called "Astro for Kids."

National Aeronautics and Space Administration (NASA), Sun for Kids (www.nasa.gov/vision/universe/solarsys tem/sun_for_kids_main.html). Describes what the Sun is, why it changes, how hot it is, and how old it is. The site includes many pictures, as well as videoclips, games, and activities.

Stanford Solar Center (http://solar-center.stanford.edu/ about.html). Kids can find almost anything they want to know about the Sun in this excellent site. Includes many facts about the Sun, photographs, and fun interactive features such as "Hear the Sun Sing" and "Watch the Sun Move."

Windows to the Universe (www.windows.ucar.edu). An informative site with a special section on the Sun. Features news stories, photographs, games, and activities for kids.

Yahoo Kids Science (http://kids.yahoo.com/science). Includes an excellent collection of information about the solar system, the Sun and other stars, eclipses, and other solar phenomena. Also features areas called "Science joke" and "Earl answers your science questions."

Index

Ahrens, Donald, 22
Antarctica (South Pole), 17
Arctic (North Pole), 17
Atmosphere
  of Earth, 15
  of Sun, 6–10
Auroras, 24–26

Chromosphere, 8, 9
Convective zone, 5
Core, 5
  demise of Sun and, 37, 39
  nuclear fusion in, 8
Corona, 8, 9, 28, 36
  temperature of, 9–10

Differential rotation, 10

Earth
  observations of Sun from,
    31–33
  Sun and climate of, 14–16
  Sun and life on, 12–14
  tilt of, 17

Fisher, Dick, 37
Food chain, 13–14, 14

Galileo Galilei, 30

Greenhouse effect, 15
Guhathakurta, Madhulika,
  30

Heliocentric theory, 30
Hinode (spacecraft), 34,
  36–37

Mercury, 18–19

National Solar Observatory,
  32
Nebulas, 4, 5
Neptune, 18
North Pole (Arctic), 17
Northern Lights (aurora
  borealis), 24, 26
Nuclear fusion, 8

Oceans, 16

Photosphere, 6–7, 39
  temperature of, 9
Photosynthesis, 13
Plants
  effects of sunlight on, 13

Rainbows, 22, 23
Red giants, 39

Solar and Heliospheric
  Observatory (SOHO),
  33–34, 35
Solar eclipses, 26–29
Solar system, 6, 11, 31
  role of Sun in, 10
Solar wind (solar flares), 26,
  27
South Pole (Antarctica), 17
Southern Lights, 24
Sun, 36
  atmosphere of, 6–10
  birth of, 4
  color of sky and, 20–22
  distance from earth, 4
  lifespan of, 37
  observations of, from

Earth, 31–33
  rotation of, 10
  size and composition of,
  5–7
  space-based studies of,
  33–34, 36–37
  temperatures in, 8
  worship of, 12
Sun dogs, 24, 25
Sun halos, 24
Sunspots, 7, 7, 25, 32

Tsunami, solar, 32, 32–33

Venus, 19

White dwarves, 38, 39

Picture Credits

Cover photo: photos.com
AP Images, 25, 28, 36
Michael P. Gadomski/Photo Researchers, Inc., 23
© The Gale Group, 13, 14
Mark Garlick/Photo Researchers, Inc., 38
Ton Kinsbergen/Photo Researchers, Inc., 35
Larry Landolfi/Photo Researchers, Inc., 21
National Aeronautics and Space Administration, 5, 6, 9
National Aeronautics and Space Administration/Photo
   Researchers Inc., 27
© National Aeronautics Space Administration/Jet
   Propulsion Laboratory/Caltech, 18
Calvin Nicholls/Stock Illustration Source/Getty Images,
   11
Pekka Parviatnen/Photo Researchers, Inc., 26
Photo Researchers, Inc., 7
Science Source/Photo Researchers, Inc., 32
Sheila Terry/Photo Researchers, Inc., 31
© Bruno P. Zehnder/Peter Arnold, Inc., 16

Peggy J. Parks holds a bachelor of science degree from Aquinas College in Grand Rapids, Michigan, where she graduated magna cum laude. She is a freelance author who has written more than 60 nonfiction books for children and young adults. Parks lives in Muskegon, Michigan, a town that she says inspires her writing because of its location on the shores of Lake Michigan.